Alexander Astremsky

STORY-FLASH

WORKBOOK

STORY-FLASH.COM

Contents

About The Author 6
About The Workbook 7
25 Reasons to Use the Workbook 9
Idea to be Developed 13
Section 1. Story Development 14
Checklist #1 Steps of Creating the Story 14
    Step 1. Describe the Primary Situation 17
    Step 2. Create the Protagonist 18
    Step 3. Describe the Knowledge, Skills and Abilities of your Protagonist 19
    Step 4. Give the protagonist some tools 20
    Step 5. Devise the Emotional Wound for the Protagonist 21
    Step 6. Give the protagonist a flaw 22
    Step 7. Create the Main Antagonist 23
    Step 8. Endow the antagonist with power 24
    Step 9. Describe Why the Antagonist Opposes the Protagonist 25
    Step 10. Describe Various Kinds of Problems, Obstacles and Difficulties 26
    Step 11. Develop the Other Characters 27
    Step 12. Each Story Has Three Parts 28
    Step 13. Think of a Few Minor Conflicts 31
    Step 14. Think of Several Ways to Make the Audience Dislike the Antagonist 32
    Step 15. Describe How You Will Punish the Antagonist at the End of the Story 33
    Step 16. Describe How You Will Reward the Protagonist at the End of the Movie 34
    Step 17. Determine What Will Happen to the Protagonist if he Does Not Reach His Goal 35
    Step 18. Describe How the Protagonist Will Change 36

- Step 19. Create the secondary line 37
- Step 20. Identify the person 38
- Step 21. Create a Mysterious and Exciting Legend 39

Section 2. Creating TheEpisode Plan 40
Checklist #2. The Episode Plan Technology 41
- Step 0. Describe The Story 44
- Step 1. Create The Exposition 46
- Step 2. Create The Inciting Incident 48
- Step3. Work On The Orientation Period 50
- Step 4. Develop The First Plot Point 52
- Step 5. Work On The Adjustment Period 54
- Step 6. Develop The Main Turning Point 56
- Step 7. Work Out The Action Period 58
- Step 8. Develop The Second Plot Point 60
- Step 9. Work Out The Protagonist's Crisis 62
- Step 10. Create The Final Battle 64
- Step 11. Create The Climax 66
- Step 12. Describe The Resolution 68
- Step 13. Create The Timeline 70
- Step 14. Divide The Story Into Episodes 74
- Step 15. Ensure Having The Elements That Advance The Plot 76
- Step 16. Make The List of All Episodes And Name Them 78

Section 3. Character Development 80
Checklist #3.The Character Development Technology 81
Character #1_____ 82
- Step 1. Determine the Character's Function 82
- Step 2. Set an Exact Goal For the Character 84
- Step 3. Describe the Character's Motivation 86
- Step 4. Develop Your Character's "Heaven" 88
- Step 5. Develop Your Character's "Hell" 89
- Step 6. Create the Emotional Wound 90

Step 7. Devise the Internal Conflict 91
Step 8. Describe the Character's Strengths..................................92
Step 9. Describe the Character's Weaknesses........................93
Step 10. Create the Character's Special Characteristics.........94
Step 11. Create the Character's External Image 96
Step 12. Work out the character's Conflicts 97
Step 13. Work out the character's personal Growth 98

Character #2 _____ 100
Step 1. Determine the Character's Function 100
Step 2. Set an exact Goal For the Character.........................101
Step 3. Describe the Character's Motivation 102
Step 4. Develop your character's "Heaven" 104
Step 5. Develop Your Character's "Hell" 105
Step 6. Create the Emotional Wound...................................106
Step 7. Devise the Internal Conflict..107
Step 8. Describe the Character's Strengths.........................108
Step 9. Describe the character's Weaknesses 109
Step 10. Create the Character's Special Characteristics.........110
Step 11. Create the Character's External Image 112
Step 12. Work Out the Character's Conflicts 113
Step 13. Work Out the Character's Personal Growth 114

Character #3_____ 116
Step 1. Determine the Character's Function 116
Step 2. Set an Exact Goal For the Character.........................117
Step 3. Describe the Character's Motivation........................118
Step 4. Develop your character's "Heaven" 120
Step 5. Develop your Character's "Hell" 121
Step 6. Create the Emotional Wound 122
Step 7. Devise the Internal Conflict..123
Step 8. Describe the character's Strengths.........................124
Step 9. Describe the character's Weaknesses 125

- Step 10. Create the Character's Special Characteristics 126
- Step 11. Create the character's External Image 128
- Step 12. Work out the character's CONFLICTS 129
- Step 13. Work out the character's personal GROWTH 130

Section 4. How to Make The Story As Completing As Possible 132

Checklist #4. Making The Story Compelling...................132
- Step 1. Ask The "MAIN QUESTION" 135
- Step 2. Create The "MYSTERY HOOKS" 139
- Step 3. Create The "KEYS" 143
- Step 4. Create Complicated Ways of Obtaining The "KEYS".146
- Step 5. Devise The "Increasing Pressure of The Circumstances" 149
- Step 6. Introduce Surprises And Unexpected Twists Into The Story...153

Notes and Additional Ideas 155

About The Author

Alexander Astremsky is a writer, screenwriter, author of the science fiction series *Intangibleworld*, and an economic novel and board games *Money Rules*. He is also the owner of Astremsky Marketing, a company that operates in five countries and develops presentation materials and corporate magazines. Alexander is a professional speaker and the author of online articles on plot development read by over 500 thousand people.

© 2018 Alexander Astremsky. "Story-Flash Workbook". All rights are reserved and protected by copyright law. No part of this book may be copied or reproduced in any form or by whatever means – electronic, mechanical, including photocopying, recording, posting on the Internet and corporate networks for private and public usage – without written permission, with the exception for brief quotation in critical articles and reviews. Coordinated usage of material is made with the author.

About The Workbook

The steps of this workbook are part of the Story-Flash technology described by Alexander Astremsky in his book Story-Flash: Step-by-Step Technology of Plot Development.

The workbook is meant to be used to develop the screenplays "on paper," not in front of the screen. Take it with you to the park, on a business trip, use it on the plane or at the beach. It is also perfect for those times when you are tired from constantly looking at the screen.

The workbook will enable you to develop the plot with the help of the exact technology without having to consult this book every time. To use it, simply write down the IDEA and then build up your story from there, step-by-step. From the moment you wrote down the primary situation and created the protagonist and antagonist, you can move forward without any stops until your story is built from A to Z.

The first section of the workbook allows you to create the nucleus that you will use to build the plot. The second section helps you build the structure. By doing the steps of the third section you will develop memorable and three-dimensional characters. And the fourth section will help you add tension to the story so that the readers (or viewers) cannot tear themselves away from it.

By the way, I think it's a good idea to have as many such workbooks as you have ideas in your head! That way you can easily make each of them into a finished story!

25 Reasons To Use The Workbook

1. With this Workbook, you can transfer all your ideas onto paper step by step.

2. This is a proven approach to the plot development.

3. You will not be distracted by messengers and social networks.

4. You can work on several Workbooks simultaneously and develop several stories at once.

5. The Workbook will not let a single idea of yours fall through the cracks.

6. You immediately know which section to use to write down your ideas.

7. You can take it with you to the park, on a business trip, use it on an airplane or at the beach.

8. It includes all the steps of the **Story-Flash** *technology described in this book.*

9. The Workbook will be your guide in developing the story and its characters.

10. It will be helpful to those who are new to screenwriting (or writing) as well as to professionals.

11. *This is the best way to focus on the task of developing a story.*

12. *It is perfect for use when you are away from your computer or tired of constantly looking at the screen.*

13. *You can always keep it handy.*

14. *It is great for children or teenagers who want to write stories or books, but do not know where to start.*

15. *You will always be ready for a flash of inspiration.*

16. *This Workbook will help you develop the plot quicker than you've ever imagined.*

17. *Writer's block becomes a thing of the past because now you always know what the next step is in the development of your story.*

18. *You will forget what it means to have no inspiration.*

19. *This is your partner in the plot development. Together you can make the story so profound and multifaceted that it would be possible to write a script or a novel based on it.*

20. *You will completely eliminate the confusion in your head.*

21. *You can transfer all your ideas onto paper and get a clear structure for your plot.*

22. You will have a strong plot with no "holes" or "inconsistencies."

23. The Workbook is going to save you from weeks of "the throes of writing."

24. It will save your precious time.

25. It will let you use your imagination to the fullest extent!

All the steps in the *Story-Flash* system reinforce and complement each other. Follow it page by page, write line after line, and very soon you will have a finished story!

Story-Flash System

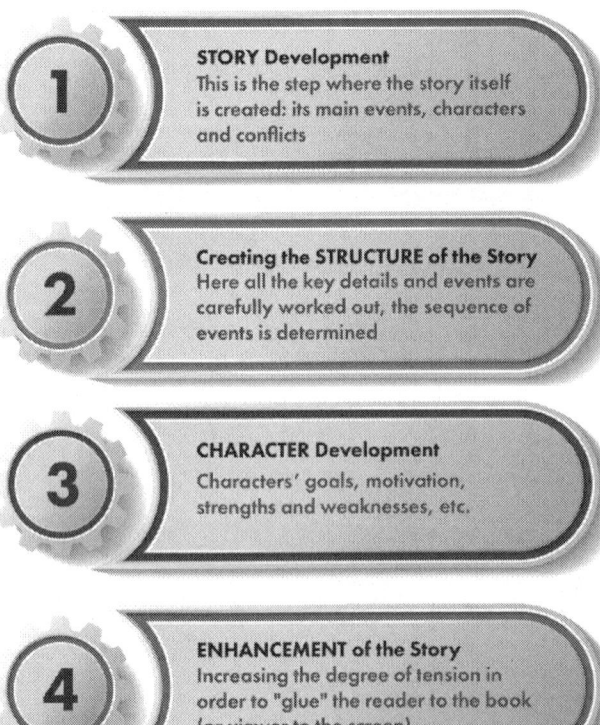

Idea To Be Developed

Section 1. Story Development

Checklist #1 Steps of Creating the Story

Step 1. In a few sentences, describe the PRIMARY SITUATION, in which the protagonist has found himself and which he must successfully handle.

Step 2. Create the PROTAGONIST. Here is what you need to know at this stage of your work: the character must be created based on his *goals* and *intentions*.

Step 3. Describe the knowledge, skills and abilities of your protagonist (everything related to his ability to confront the challenges and solve problems).

Step 4. Give the protagonist some tools that will help him achieve his goals (it can be a device, gadget or weapon).

Step 5. Devise the emotional wound for the protagonist.

Step 6. Give the protagonist a flaw. This is something that could mess up his plans, something that could jeopardize his victory.

Step 7. Now, create **the main ANTAGONIST.** It's a person (or creature) who will oppose the protagonist. Create him based on his goals and intentions.

Step 8. Endow the antagonist with power. He needs to look invincible, be unpredictable, cunning and talented.

Step 9. Describe why the antagonist opposes the protagonist. The main CONFLICT of the script should become very apparent in this step.

Step 10. Describe various kinds of problems, obstacles and difficulties that the antagonist could create for the main character.

Step 11. Develop the other characters (him based on their goals and intentions). They can be divided into protagonist's friends and enemies.

Step 12. EACH STORY HAS THREE PARTS: the beginning, the middle part and the end. After completing all the previous steps, you can describe each part of the script in a few sentences.

Step 13. Think of a few minor conflicts.

Step 14. Think of several ways to **make the audience dislike the antagonist.**

STEP 15. Describe how you will punish the antagonist at the end of the story.

Step 16. Describe how you will reward the protagonist at the end of the movie. What will he receive as a result of his victory?

Step 17. Determine what will happen to the protagonist if he does not reach his goal. This is the threat that is hanging over the main character throughout the story, getting more real and more dangerous with each page.

Step 18. Describe how the protagonist will change.

Step 19. Create the secondary line — another (secondary) storyline involving either the protagonist or the antagonist.

Step 20. Identify the person from whom the main character can learn something.

Step 21. Create a mysterious and exciting LEGEND (in other words – the background or context). It could be some kind of a myth, something that happened much earlier than the current scene.

Step 1. Describe The Primary Situation

In a few sentences, describe the PRIMARY SITUATION, in which the protagonist has found himself and which he must successfully handle. The primary situation is what the whole story is built around.

Step 2. Create The Protagonist

Here is what you need to know at this stage of your work: the character must be created based on his *goals* and *intentions*. We can say a lot about his attitudes and hobbies, but the most important thing right now is the goal he will be pursuing throughout your story.

Step 3. Describe The Knowledge, Skills and Abilities of Your Protagonist

Describe the knowledge, skills and abilities of your protagonist (everything related to his ability to confront the challenges and solve problems).

Step 4. Give The Protagonist Some Tools

Give the protagonist some tools that will help him achieve his goals (it can be a device, gadget or weapon).

Step 5. Devise The Emotional Wound For The Protagonist

As you work on your story, devise the emotional wound for the protagonist: what troubles him, what prevents him from being happy. This makes the character real, complex and relatable for the audience, otherwise, he will remain "raw" and superficial.

Step 6. Give The protagonist a Flaw

Give the protagonist a flaw. This is something that could mess up his plans, something that could jeopardize his victory.

Step 7. Create The Main Antagonist

Now, create the main ANTAGONIST. It's a person (or creature) who will oppose the protagonist. Create him as described in step 2.

Step 8. Endow The Antagonist with Power

Endow the antagonist with power. He needs to look invincible, be unpredictable, cunning and talented.

Step 9. Describe Why the Antagonist Opposes the Protagonist

Describe why the antagonist opposes the protagonist. The main CONFLICT of the script should become very apparent in this step. This is the central tension that will continue to grow and at the end of the movie will burst into flames, putting the protagonist's life and future on the line.

Step 10. Describe Various Kinds of Problems, Obstacles And Difficulties

Describe various kinds of problems, obstacles and difficulties that the antagonist could create for the main character.

Step 11. Develop The Other Characters

Develop the other characters as described in step 2. They can be divided into protagonist's friends and enemies. Each of them is going to make a difference in some way. By definition, friends help the hero achieve his objectives while the enemies interfere.

Step 12. Each Story Has Three Parts

EACH STORY HAS THREE PARTS: the beginning, the middle part and the end. After completing all the previous steps, you can describe each part of the script in a few sentences. In this step it is especially important to decide on the ending. Knowing exactly what the end of the story is going to be is one of the secrets to developing the WHOLE story effectively.

Beginning:

Middle Part:

End:

Step 13. Think Of a Few Minor Conflicts

In step 9 we've examined the main conflict of the story. Now think of a few minor conflicts.

Step 14. Think of Several Ways to Make the Audience Dislike the Antagonist

Think of several ways to make the audience dislike the antagonist: how he should act and what he has to do for that to happen.

Step 15. Describe How You Will Punish the Antagonist At The End Of The Story

Describe how you will punish the antagonist at the end of the story. The punishment must be powerful enough to make the audience rejoice when it happens. The better you do the previous step (make the audience dislike him), the happier your viewers will be.

Step 16. Describe How You Will Reward The Protagonist At The End Of The Movie

Describe how you will reward the protagonist at the end of the movie. What will he receive as a result of his victory?

Step 17. Determine What Will Happen to The Protagonist If He Does Not Reach His Goal

Determine what will happen to the protagonist if he does not reach his goal. This is the threat that is hanging over the main character throughout the story, getting more real and more dangerous with each page.

Step 18. Describe How the Protagonist Will Change

Describe how the protagonist will change. This step may not be necessary for every story or script, but the "hero's change" is one of the secrets to invoking POWERFUL EMOTIONS in your audience and creating a lasting impression from the story.

Step 19. Create The Secondary Line

Create the secondary line — another (secondary) storyline involving either the protagonist or the antagonist. This is one of the ways to give your story additional depth.

Step 20. Identify The Person

Identify the person (or thing) from whom the main character can learn something. That is, there should be a person (or a creature) that will help our protagonist use his abilities better and overcome the obstacles more efficiently.

Step 21. Create a Mysterious And Exciting Legend

Create a mysterious and exciting LEGEND (in other words – the background or context). It could be some kind of a myth, something that happened much earlier than the current scene, but without it, the events described in the story would not be as exciting and fascinating. A good, strong LEGEND is one of the main secrets to having the audience completely immersed in the story.

Section 2. Creating The Episode Plan

Checklist #2. The Episode Plan Technology

Step 1. Create The Exposition

Step 2. Create The Inciting Incident

Step 3. Work On The Orientation Period

Step 4. Develop The First Plot Point

Step 5. Work On The Adjustment Period

Step 6. Develop The Main Turning Point

Step 7. Work Out The Action Period

Step 8. Develop The Second Plot Point

Step 9. Work Out The Protagonist's Crisis

Step 10. Create The Final Battle

Step 11. Create The Climax

Step 12. Describe The Resolution

IMPORTANT: Here is what needs to happen after the climax:

1. The main character and (or) those affected by his victory need to understand what it means for them. Give the audience a taste of the win and show the joy!

2. You need to show that the victory is final, and the evil is not likely to return (at least soon).

3. Then show how the life of the protagonist and (or) his team has changed after the evil was defeated.

4. Finally, the resolution's most important point – the demonstration of the hero's ideals that are now a reality.

Step 13. Create The Timeline

Step 14. Divide The Story Into Episodes

Step 15. Ensure Having The Elements That Advance The Plot

Step 16. Make The List of All Episodes And Name Them

STORY-FLASH. The Storyline Structure: 12 Components

Step 1 — Story-Flash Structure	Step 2 — Story-Flash Structure	Step 3 — Story-Flash Structure
THE EXPOSITION	THE INCITING INCIDENT	THE ORIENTATION PERIOD
0-10 %	10 %	10-25 %

Step 4 — Story-Flash Structure	Step 5 — Story-Flash Structure	Step 6 — Story-Flash Structure
THE FIRST PLOT POINT	THE ADJUSTMENT PERIOD	THE MAIN TURNING POINT
25 %	25-50 %	50 %

Step 7 — Story-Flash Structure	Step 8 — Story-Flash Structure	Step 9 — Story-Flash Structure
THE ACTION PERIOD	THE SECOND PLOT POINT	THE PROTAGONIST'S CRISIS
50-75 %	75 %	Between 75-95 %

Step 10 — Story-Flash Structure	Step 11 — Story-Flash Structure	Step 12 — Story-Flash Structure
THE FINAL BATTLE	THE CLIMAX	THE RESOLUTION
Between 75-95 %	End of the final battle	95-100 %

Creating The Episode Plan

Step 0. Describe The Story

After you have done the steps from the previous chapter, describe the story you have developed as fully as you can. All further actions will make it more profound and organized, step by step. Do not worry if you'll have to not only expand but also re-work some events. This is a part of the process that gives your story depth and dimension.

Step 1. Create The Exposition

In the first half of the first act we have the "exposition" or, simply put, the opening.

Definition of exposition: an introductory part of a literary or musical piece containing the motifs that will be developed further.

Here you should show the audience the protagonist's life, his environment and his challenges. You need to get the viewer to take a liking to your main character.

Step 2. Create The Inciting Incident

The inciting incident usually concludes the exposition. Approximately 10 percent into the story, the main character must find himself in some sort of a situation that will show the viewer where the whole story is going. The inciting incident creates the impulse that propels the protagonist into another world, a new adventure or some unexpected trouble.

Step3. Work On The Orientation Period

After the exposition and before the first plot point, there is a period when the protagonist gets oriented in the new environment (where he wound up due to the inciting incident). At the same time, we should also orient the AUDIENCE as to where the protagonist is, his surroundings, existing threats in his environment, and what will happen if the evil wins. By "evil" here we mean something that prevents the main character from having a happy life and what stands in the way of achieving his goals.

Step 4. Develop The First Plot Point

It takes place at the end of the first act, approximately one quarter into the story. This is the transition from the first act into the second. This is a place where something makes the protagonist go along a certain way or pushes him to make a decision that the audience was not expecting. This is the moment when the main character STARTS on the way that should lead him to his goal. Here you need to set the exact direction for all further developments and events.

Step 5. Work On The Adjustment Period

Between the first plot point and the main turning point, there is an adjustment period. For the next 25 percent (one quarter) of your story, the main character adjusts to the circumstances resulting from the first plot point. He tries to predict the future events, makes plans to achieve his objective and prepares for action.

In this step you also need to describe what the antagonist and (or) his supporters are doing meanwhile.

Step 6. Develop The Main Turning Point

Approximately in the middle of the story there is the so-called main turning point. This is the moment when the protagonist becomes more of a master of the situation rather than a person who is going with the flow. His chances of winning increase thanks to his new knowledge, skills or abilities. Now he is 100 percent sure that he can reach his goal. Often this is the moment when the hero "burns all the bridges," and the viewers realize that there is no turning back. The motto is "Never look back!"

Step 7. Work Out The Action Period

Between the main turning point and the second plot point, the main character and his team are proactive and deliberate in their fight with evil. This is the second half of the second act and this part of the script has the most intense action for both positive and negative characters.

Write down the actions of the main character and the members of his team; then describe the dirty deeds of the antagonist and his supporters at this point of the story.

The key to doing this step correctly is the understanding of the principle "every action has an equal and opposite reaction;" in other words, when the protagonist moves forward — the antagonist pushes him back. The size of the goal determines the size of the obstacles and challenges on the way towards it. It is the law of life and the law of creating a great story.

Step 8. Develop The Second Plot Point

Mr. "Second Act" brought a lot of trouble to our protagonist and gave him a really rough time on his way to the goal. But now the main problems are behind him (or so he thinks) and the victory is close ... He has to take just one more step, open the last door, pull the trigger and ... all of a sudden, there is the second plot point. THE PLAN HAS FAILED!!! The smell of victory disappears and gets replaced by the stench of the villain who pins our hero against the wall with all his might. We can call this moment a "big failure." This is the transition to the third act.

The second plot point acts as a catalyst for tension and conflict. It makes the protagonist take the most drastic measures here and now. After all, he did not give up! The goal can still be achieved! Thus, the second plot point puts the protagonist in a situation where he has to make one last decisive effort to win or die in the attack.

Step 9. Work Out The Protagonist's Crisis

In order to win, you have to look inside yourself and reconsider some of your views or ideas. After all, something has brought the protagonist to failure or gave him big problems (either wrong ideas or his modus operandi). So if he gets to the bottom of his fears, doubts, weaknesses or mistakes … he can still win. Here is the principle used by wise people striving for their goals, "If my plan has failed, that means something needs to be changed." Most often, it concerns one's own modus operandi or views on life. Hence, here comes the "protagonist's crisis."

This is the biggest test for the hero's character, a review of established principles or return to his lost ideals. The crisis poses a difficult choice for the main character, and this is the critical moment in the story. This episode shows us whether the protagonist gave up or remained unwavering, whether he started fully believing in himself or could not overcome his weaknesses. This crisis can happen right before the final battle (see the following step) or even in the middle of it.

Step 10. Create The Final Battle

From the second plot point on, the main character will have to give it his all so that despite everything, he can still achieve his goal. The chance of winning is minimal, the risk and conflict are at their highest, and the protagonist enters the final battle with the antagonist.

During the final battle the audience should feel that everything is working against the protagonist and that he is about to lose or die. Often it is the most emotional moment of the story due to the fullest manifestation of good and evil. By the way, if we show that the protagonist was able to defeat evil because of his internal change, the viewer can experience a real emotional outburst.

Step 11. Create The Climax

*Definition of the word **climax**: a point of the highest tension, enthusiasm, development of something.*

The final battle ends with the climax. This is the moment of liberation, the triumph of the principles embodied by the main character in his actions. And of course, it is the final victory, everything he fought for so hard right to the very end (this victory, mind you, could have been won at the cost of his own life). The climax occurs between approximately the 90 percent mark of the story and the last several minutes.

Step 12. Describe The Resolution

The resolution is the part of the script located between the climax and the words "The End." Professional creation of resolutions is a true art. It is worth mastering, of course, if you don't want people to say that the endings of your scripts are weak.

Here is what needs to happen after the climax:

1. The main character and (or) those affected by his victory need to understand what it means for them. Give the audience a taste of the win and show the joy!

2. You need to show that the victory is final, and the evil is not likely to return (at least soon).

3. Then show how the life of the protagonist and (or) his team has changed after the evil was defeated.

4. Finally, the resolution's most important point – the demonstration of the hero's ideals that are now a reality.

These four points give the movie a sense of completeness, and the viewer leaves the movie theatre very satisfied.

Step 13. Create The Timeline

The timeline is an auxiliary tool that is a MAP of the sequence of events.

By now your story should have taken a complete form, but you may still have some confusion in your thoughts. To handle it, I strongly recommend doing the following:

a) Take three A4-size sheets of paper and glue them together so that you get a long landscape sheet (3x longer than a standard sheet).

b) Draw a horizontal line on the paper that goes through all three sheets. This will be the movie's timeline.

c) Draw seven "flags" or seven vertical bars on this line and mark them as follows: the opening, the inciting event (10 percent from the beginning), the first plot point (25 percent), the main turning point (50 percent), the second plot point (75 percent), the climax (at any point between the 90 and 99 percent) and the end.

d) Now put the glued sheets vertically so that the flag for the opening is at the top.

e) Take a pen or a pencil and consecutively describe all

the events you have developed by now locating them on the timeline between the flags.

The mathematical accuracy of placing the events is not too significant here; what's important is that you transfer the key points of the story onto the timeline (on the paper, that is).

This is an excellent remedy for the confusion in your head. Try it!

Step 14. Divide The Story Into Episodes

An episode is a series of scenes united by a common location or subject. In other words, an episode consists of scenes, not vice versa.

A scene is a separate part of the action. In our case, it's a part of an episode.

Each episode is a small story that has a beginning, middle part, and the end. For example, if the main character took three minutes to go to the store to get some bread, it can be considered an episode. However, his banter with the saleswoman in the store is a scene (one minute). The moment when he met his classmate Maria on his way back home could be another scene (one minute). So "going out to get bread — buying bread — coming back" is an episode and the events taking place during his "trip to get the bread" are scenes.

Each episode usually takes about three minutes (but this is not a strict rule). Now, after all the work that you've done, you'll need to divide the story into approximately 40 parts to make the episode plan. The timeline tool will help you see the parts (episodes) that your story consists of.

Step 15. Ensure Having The Elements That Advance The Plot

Each episode should actively move the story forward. Therefore, in this step go through all the episodes sequentially and make sure each of them has the elements that advance the plot.

An element that advances the plot is the point that makes the story DEVELOP.

Step 16. Make The List Of All Episodes And Name Them

Many people write the to-do lists to increase their productivity (what should be done, plan for the week, etc.). This helps concentrate on the tasks and goals.

Now that your episode plan is done, I recommend you make a list of episodes and give them short titles. This will be your "to-do list." Print it out and hang over your table. When you work on the script, you will move forward according to this list. And believe me, you will experience great satisfaction when you check the item off this plan after you finalize that episode in your work.

Section 3. Character Development

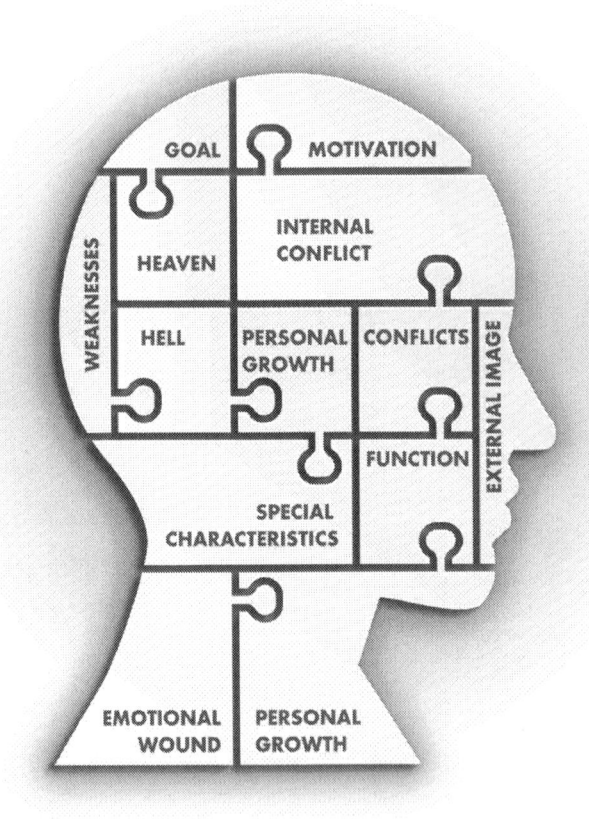

- GOAL
- MOTIVATION
- WEAKNESSES
- HEAVEN
- INTERNAL CONFLICT
- HELL
- PERSONAL GROWTH
- CONFLICTS
- EXTERNAL IMAGE
- FUNCTION
- SPECIAL CHARACTERISTICS
- EMOTIONAL WOUND
- PERSONAL GROWTH

Checklist #3. The Character Development Technology

Step 1. Determine the character's FUNCTION

Step 2. Set an exact GOAL for the character

Step 3. Describe the character's MOTIVATION

Step 4. Develop your character's "HEAVEN"

Step 5. Develop your character's "HELL"

Step 6. Create the EMOTIONAL WOUND

Step 7. Devise the INTERNAL CONFLICT

Step 8. Describe the character's STRENGTHS

Step 9. Describe the character's WEAKNESSES

Step 10. Create the character's SPECIAL CHARACTERISTICS

Step 11. Create the character's EXTERNAL IMAGE

Step 12. Work out the character's CONFLICTS

Step 13. Work out the character's PERSONAL GROWTH

Character Development

Character #1_____

Step 1. Determine The Character's Function

The starting point that all the subsequent steps will be based on is the character's FUNCTION.

Ask yourself the following questions:

1. Is the character's intention to HELP the protagonist reach his main goal or PREVENT him from that?

2. How is he going to pursue his intentions?

3. What is his role in the story?

Step 2. Set an Exact Goal For The Character

After you've determined the character's role in your story in the previous step, you should define his **final objective** (it must be related to this story, not what he wants to achieve in life in general). Or you could determine the solution to his main problem.

When doing this step, remember that the GOAL is always something **specific** (like the key, the door, the exit, getting married, stealing the diamond, wiping the enemy off the face of the earth, etc.).

Step 3. Describe The Character's Motivation

Now find a clear motive that prompted your character to "get involved" in this story. Why, from the viewpoint of this character, must he perform his **function**?

Character's motivation is always internal. Motivation reveals his true nature and gives us a chance to see his inner world. Therefore, when developing a character, your primary task is to fully determine the MOTIVES of his ACTIONS.

Please note: motivation is not necessarily something that stays fixed throughout the story. Moreover, by changing the motivation you can clearly show the growth of your character as the story unfolds.

The key question to determine the character's motivation is: What makes him do what he does?

Step 4. Develop Your Character's "Heaven"

What are his dreams? What does he strive for? The character's "heaven" is often the same as what will happen when he reaches his goal, or when the main problem is solved.

Please note: the character's "HEAVEN" should be directly related to the events of the story, and not something generic like "becoming a millionaire" or "marrying a prince."

Step 5. Develop Your Character's "Hell"

What is his biggest fear? What is he trying to avoid at all costs? What will happen if he doesn't reach his goal or solve the main problem?

It is the situation, which he absolutely does not want to be in. Moreover, it's what could happen to him if he does not "get a move on" in the story.

Step 6. Create The Emotional Wound

Here are some types of possible emotional wounds: "I want, but I can't," "I wanted, but I failed (did not work out)" or "things are not what I thought they were." Most often, it is a conflict of desire and opportunity. It could also be a major failure in the past that affects the current life and emotional state of the character.

Step 7. Devise The Internal Conflict

Internal conflict is a conflict of the person's desires (or intentions). This is what makes the character feel the tension, doubt and uncertainty about his further actions. **This is the problem of making the right choice.**

For example: keep going towards his goal or give up? Kill the enemy or let him live? Leave her husband or accept his infidelity? Keep supporting the good cause or cross over to the dark side?

Step 8. Describe The Character's Strengths

The character's strong points are his traits, his abilities, knowledge, skills or areas of expertise that will help him reach his goals.

Step 9. Describe The Character's Weaknesses

The character's weaknesses are those flaws that will slow him down while moving towards his objective.

Step 10. Create The Character's Special Characteristics

Special characteristics are particular qualities of somebody or something. Character's special characteristics are usually developed in two stages. The first one is the creation of the internal characteristics; the second – external.

An internal characteristic is a trait, a hobby, a habit, etc., that influences the person's decisions and actions, and subsequently – the plot. An internal characteristic can be the same as one of the character's strong or weak points, or it can be a unique personality characteristic. It can frequently have a significant impact on the course of events and can lead to dramatic story twists.

An external characteristic can be any detail of the character's appearance, of his facial expressions or motions. This is something that attracts attention to the character, makes him recognizable and different from the others. For example, a tattoo, haircut, particular look in his eyes, body type, sparkly ring, strange laughter, unusual facial expressions, etc.

Step 11. Create The Character's External Image

An image is a description that creates a vivid idea about someone.

In our case, this is what the viewer will see on the screen: the appearance, style of clothing, age and other external features of the character.

Step 12. Work Out The Character's Conflicts

For the character to attract interest, it is necessary to introduce some other characters with whom he will be in conflict or have strong disagreements. A disagreement can manifest itself differently in different characters, but most often it leads to disputes, conflicts, upsets, quarrels or fights and can create a lot of either comic or tragic moments (depending on your genre). If your character is kind and not prone to conflict, well, figure out who and how will be suppressing him, who he will have to fight back if necessary, or who he will have to avoid throughout the story in order to not get into a great deal of trouble.

Step 13. Work Out The Character's Personal Growth

In a screenplay, the protagonist, as well as some supporting characters, can (and ideally will) change. This usually happens when the character overcomes his weaknesses and acquires strengths. It may also be a change in the character's motivation or his philosophy and attitudes towards life. As a rule, the character's personal growth directly affects the development of the story (to get a better understanding of this – see the previous two chapters).

The key to the personal development is making the character grow and show "what he is made of" as a result of what happens to him in the story.

Character #2 _____

Step 1. Determine The Character's Function

The starting point that all the subsequent steps will be based on is the character's FUNCTION.

Ask yourself the following questions:

1. Is the character's intention to HELP the protagonist reach his main goal or PREVENT him from that?

2. How is he going to pursue his intentions?

3. What is his role in the story?

Step 2. Set an Exact Goal For The Character

After you've determined the character's role in your story in the previous step, you should define his **final objective** (it must be related to this story, not what he wants to achieve in life in general). Or you could determine the solution to his main problem.

When doing this step, remember that the GOAL is always something **specific** (like the key, the door, the exit, getting married, stealing the diamond, wiping the enemy off the face of the earth, etc.).

Step 3. Describe The Character's Motivation

Now find a clear motive that prompted your character to "get involved" in this story. Why, from the viewpoint of this character, must he perform his **function**?

Character's motivation is always internal. Motivation reveals his true nature and gives us a chance to see his inner world. Therefore, when developing a character, your primary task is to fully determine the MOTIVES of his ACTIONS.

Please note: motivation is not necessarily something that stays fixed throughout the story. Moreover, by changing the motivation you can clearly show the growth of your character as the story unfolds.

The key question to determine the character's motivation is: What makes him do what he does?

Step 4. Develop Your Character's "Heaven"

What are his dreams? What does he strive for? The character's "heaven" is often the same as what will happen when he reaches his goal, or when the main problem is solved.

Please note: the character's "HEAVEN" should be directly related to the events of the story, and not something generic like "becoming a millionaire" or "marrying a prince."

Step 5. Develop Your Character's "Hell"

What is his biggest fear? What is he trying to avoid at all costs? What will happen if he doesn't reach his goal or solve the main problem?

It is the situation, which he absolutely does not want to be in. Moreover, it's what could happen to him if he does not "get a move on" in the story.

Step 6. Create The Emotional Wound

Here are some types of possible emotional wounds: "I want, but I can't," "I wanted, but I failed (did not work out)" or "things are not what I thought they were." Most often, it is a conflict of desire and opportunity. It could also be a major failure in the past that affects the current life and emotional state of the character.

Step 7. Devise The Internal Conflict

Internal conflict is a conflict of the person's desires (or intentions). This is what makes the character feel the tension, doubt and uncertainty about his further actions. **This is the problem of making the right choice.**

For example: keep going towards his goal or give up? Kill the enemy or let him live? Leave her husband or accept his infidelity? Keep supporting the good cause or cross over to the dark side?

Step 8. Describe The Character's Strengths

The character's strong points are his traits, his abilities, knowledge, skills or areas of expertise that will **help** him reach his goals.

Step 9. Describe The Character's Weaknesses

The character's weaknesses are those flaws that will **slow him down** while moving towards his objective.

Step 10. Create The Character's Special Characteristics

Special characteristics are particular qualities of somebody or something. Character's special characteristics are usually developed in two stages. The first one is the creation of the internal characteristics; the second – external.

An internal characteristic is a trait, a hobby, a habit, etc., that influences the person's decisions and actions, and subsequently – the plot. An internal characteristic can be the same as one of the character's strong or weak points, or it can be a unique personality characteristic. It can frequently have a significant impact on the course of events and can lead to dramatic story twists.

An external characteristic can be any detail of the character's appearance, of his facial expressions or motions. This is something that attracts attention to the character, makes him recognizable and different from the others. For example, a tattoo, haircut, particular look in his eyes, body type, sparkly ring, strange laughter, unusual facial expressions, etc.

Step 11. Create The Character's External Image

An image *is a description that creates a vivid idea about someone.*

In our case, this is what the viewer will see on the screen: the appearance, style of clothing, age and other external features of the character.

Step 12. Work Out The Character's Conflicts

For the character to attract interest, it is necessary to introduce some other characters with whom he will be in conflict or have strong disagreements. A disagreement can manifest itself differently in different characters, but most often it leads to disputes, conflicts, upsets, quarrels or fights and can create a lot of either comic or tragic moments (depending on your genre). If your character is kind and not prone to conflict, well, figure out who and how will be suppressing him, who he will have to fight back if necessary, or who he will have to avoid throughout the story in order to not get into a great deal of trouble.

Step 13. Work Out The Character's Personal Growth

In a screenplay, the protagonist, as well as some supporting characters, can (and ideally will) change. This usually happens when the character overcomes his weaknesses and acquires strengths. It may also be a change in the character's motivation or his philosophy and attitudes towards life. As a rule, the character's personal growth directly affects the development of the story (to get a better understanding of this – see the previous two chapters).

The key to the personal development is making the character grow and show "what he is made of" as a result of what happens to him in the story.

Character #3 _____

Step 1. Determine The Character's Function

The starting point that all the subsequent steps will be based on is the character's FUNCTION.

Ask yourself the following questions:

1. Is the character's intention to HELP the protagonist reach his main goal or PREVENT him from that?

2. How is he going to pursue his intentions?

3. What is his role in the story?

Step 2. Set an Exact Goal For The Character

After you've determined the character's role in your story in the previous step, you should define his **final objective** (it must be related to this story, not what he wants to achieve in life in general). Or you could determine the solution to his main problem.

When doing this step, remember that the GOAL is always something **specific** (like the key, the door, the exit, getting married, stealing the diamond, wiping the enemy off the face of the earth, etc.).

Step 3. Describe The Character's Motivation

Now find a clear motive that prompted your character to "get involved" in this story. Why, from the viewpoint of this character, must he perform his **function**?

Character's motivation is always internal. Motivation reveals his true nature and gives us a chance to see his inner world. Therefore, when developing a character, your primary task is to fully determine the MOTIVES of his ACTIONS.

Please note: motivation is not necessarily something that stays fixed throughout the story. Moreover, by changing the motivation you can clearly show the growth of your character as the story unfolds.

The key question to determine the character's motivation is: What makes him do what he does?

Step 4. Develop your Character's "Heaven"

What are his dreams? What does he strive for? The character's "heaven" is often the same as what will happen when he reaches his goal, or when the main problem is solved.

Please note: the character's "HEAVEN" should be directly related to the events of the story, and not something generic like "becoming a millionaire" or "marrying a prince."

Step 5. Develop your Character's "Hell"

What is his biggest fear? What is he trying to avoid at all costs? What will happen if he doesn't reach his goal or solve the main problem?

It is the situation, which he absolutely does not want to be in. Moreover, it's what could happen to him if he does not "get a move on" in the story.

Step 6. Create The Emotional Wound

Here are some types of possible emotional wounds: "I want, but I can't," "I wanted, but I failed (did not work out)" or "things are not what I thought they were." Most often, it is a conflict of desire and opportunity. It could also be a major failure in the past that affects the current life and emotional state of the character.

Step 7. Devise The Internal Conflict

Internal conflict is a conflict of the person's desires (or intentions). This is what makes the character feel the tension, doubt and uncertainty about his further actions. **This is the problem of making the right choice.**

For example: keep going towards his goal or give up? Kill the enemy or let him live? Leave her husband or accept his infidelity? Keep supporting the good cause or cross over to the dark side?

Step 8. Describe The Character's Strengths

The character's strong points are his traits, his abilities, knowledge, skills or areas of expertise that will help him reach his goals.

Step 9. Describe The Character's Weaknesses

The character's weaknesses are those flaws that will slow him down while moving towards his objective.

Step 10. Create The Character's Special Characteristics

Special characteristics are particular qualities of somebody or something. Character's special characteristics are usually developed in two stages. The first one is the creation of the internal characteristics; the second – external.

An internal characteristic is a trait, a hobby, a habit, etc., that influences the person's decisions and actions, and subsequently – the plot. An internal characteristic can be the same as one of the character's strong or weak points, or it can be a unique personality characteristic. It can frequently have a significant impact on the course of events and can lead to dramatic story twists.

An external characteristic can be any detail of the character's appearance, of his facial expressions or motions. This is something that attracts attention to the character, makes him recognizable and different from the others. For example, a tattoo, haircut, particular look in his eyes, body type, sparkly ring, strange laughter, unusual facial expressions, etc.

Step 11. Create The Character's External Image

An image is a description that creates a vivid idea about someone.

In our case, this is what the viewer will see on the screen: the appearance, style of clothing, age and other external features of the character.

Step 12. Work Out The Character's Conflicts

For the character to attract interest, it is necessary to introduce some other characters with whom he will be in conflict or have strong disagreements. A disagreement can manifest itself differently in different characters, but most often it leads to disputes, conflicts, upsets, quarrels or fights and can create a lot of either comic or tragic moments (depending on your genre). If your character is kind and not prone to conflict, well, figure out who and how will be suppressing him, who he will have to fight back if necessary, or who he will have to avoid throughout the story in order to not get into a great deal of trouble.

Step 13. Work Out The Character's Personal Growth

In a screenplay, the protagonist, as well as some supporting characters, can (and ideally will) change. This usually happens when the character overcomes his weaknesses and acquires strengths. It may also be a change in the character's motivation or his philosophy and attitudes towards life. As a rule, the character's personal growth directly affects the development of the story (to get a better understanding of this – see the previous two chapters).

The key to the personal development is making the character grow and show "what he is made of" as a result of what happens to him in the story.

Section 4. How To Make The Story As Completing As Possible

Checklist #4. Making The Story Compelling

Step 1. Ask The "Main Question"

This is the question that the viewer will try to answer throughout the whole movie.

Step 2. Create The "Mystery Hooks"

By "mystery hooks" we mean various secrets that your story needs to be packed with.

Step 3. Create The "Keys"

A "key" is the information that was obtained, the mystery that was solved or a certain object that the character needs as a "pass" for the next stage of the story.

Step 4. Create Complicated Ways Of Obtaining The "Keys"

Here's the secret. When you know exactly WHAT all the "keys" to the new levels of your story are, you can make the process of getting each key into a separate "mini-adventure." And here is another important principle: *the characters must work hard to obtain the "keys." It should not be simply "I came, I saw, I conquered." It must be difficult for them.*

Step 5. Devise The "Increasing Pressure Of The Circumstances"

Here are some ways that can help you create such "pressure" in your script:

1. **Increase the number of people who "play against" the protagonist.**

2. **Loss of tools, weapons or abilities necessary for achieving his goal** (or simply for protection) – take away any opportunity, ability or a valuable tool from the protagonist.

3. **Add something that impedes the protagonist.** For example, an injury to one of his supporters who now needs to be carried and the lack of possibility to leave him in a safe place.

4. ***Conflict with his supporters*** *(loss or departure of one or more of them).*

5. ***Increase the number of obstacles*** *(a lot of various barriers).*

6. ***Increase the difficulty of obstacles*** *(few obstacles, however, they are almost insurmountable).*

Step 6. Introduce Surprises And Unexpected Twists Into The Story

Enhancement Of The Story

Step 1. Ask The "Main Question"

It's human nature that any secret or suspense captures one's attention in some mystical way. A mystery is something that a person just can't make peace with, so one's attention will always focus on questions and uncertainties.

When we talk about using "questions" in a movie, this is the cornerstone of creating and controlling interest. Moreover, if the "principle of questions" is used correctly, you will provide the greatest enjoyment and satisfaction for your viewers.

So here is the first step: INTRODUCE THE "MAIN QUESTION" INTO THE STORY.

This is the question that the viewer will try to answer throughout the whole movie.

"How is it going to end?" "Who will be the winner?" "Who will get the first prize?" These are the kinds of questions that a screenwriter has to be able to pose in his screenplay at the very beginning of his work. If you are currently writing a screenplay, just ask yourself, "What is the 'main question' that the viewer will be trying to answer throughout the movie?"

Your answer, believe me, is worth its weight in gold. Based on the answer create a "game" of solving a mystery for the viewer for those 1.5-2 hours that he will spend in front of the screen.

While creating the "main question" you should also keep in mind the following rule: the sooner you put the main mystery in place, the faster the viewer will get involved in your story.

Step 2. Create The "Mystery Hooks"

By "mystery hooks" we mean various secrets that your story needs to be packed with. It is an excellent auxiliary tool for the scriptwriter to maintain constant interest of the viewers. It is the "hooks" that make the viewer ask himself such questions as "What's happening?", "Who has really done it, after all?" or "Did he go down the wrong path again?"... The "mystery hooks" strategically placed throughout the story keep reminding the viewer that there is still much to be revealed and many questions have not been answered yet.

For example, we can use the "hooks" to indicate that one of the characters secretly communicates with someone and nobody on his team knows about it (or, on the contrary, somebody does know about it but cannot ask directly). Who does he communicate with? Is he a traitor or is he trying to get more help? This mystery can be solved by either the viewer or one of the main characters.

Important: the "mystery hooks" introduced into the screenplay will not only captivate the viewer but will also make the viewer's mind stay alert throughout the story. Have you watched (or read) *The Da Vinci Code* or *Harry Potter*? Do you see what I mean? The viewer truly enjoys the story when we completely immerse him in the events. To achieve this effect, it is essential to provide him with the opportunity to think together with the protagonist, analyze, make guesses, solve mysteries.

And now let's get to the point, or to be more exact, to the technology. If you simply start telling the story in the tiniest of details, the viewer could get bored within the first five minutes. That's why we take a different approach — we begin the narration by hiding the key elements. However ... we also drop some hints.

Hints indirectly indicate certain facts or circumstances but do not give us the full understanding of the situation. It piques the viewer's interest to find the solution or the answer to such questions as "What is it?" or "Where will it lead?" Therefore such hints act as the main "mystery hooks" for the audience.

Step 3. Create The "Keys"

A "key" is the information that was obtained, the mystery that was solved or a certain object that the character needs as a "pass" for the next stage of the story.

In other words, the "keys" are something that allows the characters to achieve intermediate goals on their way to the desired outcome. In this step (when you are creating the "keys"), you need to fully work out what information your character will need to receive on his way to the goal, the main mysteries he will have to solve, the objects he'll need to get or the persons he'll have to ally with in order to achieve his objectives.

For example, he will need to: figure out the code to the safety deposit box; find the enemy's location; trick the antagonist's mistress into telling him the enemy's secrets, etc.

You could say that by obtaining each subsequent "key" the hero is now able to overcome the next obstacle that was stopping him before on his way to the goal.

As the characters move along the story, they must solve even bigger mysteries, obtain the information that is more valuable, gain the objects that are more meaningful to their victory. They must collect the "keys" that become more and more important to them as their quest progresses.

Step 4. Create Complicated Ways Of Obtaining The "Keys"

Here's the secret. When you know exactly WHAT all the "keys" to the new levels of your story are, you can make the process of getting each key into a separate "mini-adventure." And here is another important principle: *the characters must work hard to obtain the "keys." It should not be simply "I came, I saw, I conquered." It must be difficult for them.*

Your viewer should feel again and again throughout the film, that the protagonist is at the breaking point, that he is about to lose, that "this time he will definitely fail."

If you make sure that the characters are looking death in the eye every time they obtain another "key," the viewer (who is going to be on the edge of his seat throughout the movie) would want to embrace you at the end.

The rule of this step is: create the circumstances with the highest risk for your character because the VIEWER'S INVOLVEMENT in the story is directly proportionate to the CHARACTER'S RISK in each scene.

Step 5. Devise The "Increasing Pressure Of The Circumstances"

Your task is to inexorably increase the opposition to the protagonist and his goals every minute. The problems must become more and more complicated, and the main threat must be getting closer and closer.

To get a better understanding of how to do this step masterfully, imagine that your protagonist is running towards his GOAL down a long road. ALL the events of your story are happening to him along this road, from the exposition to the resolution. In other words, the road represents the complete path that your hero has to travel.

Now imagine that this road is held in a vise. And from the very first minutes of the movie it is slowly but continuously getting tighter and tighter. This vise would be that "ever-increasing pressure of the circumstances."

Devise some ways to create such "pressure" in your story:

1. **Increase the number of people who "play against" the protagonist**.

2. **Loss of tools, weapons or abilities necessary for achieving his goal** (or simply for protection) – take

away any opportunity, ability or a valuable tool from the protagonist.

3. **Add something that impedes the protagonist.** For example, an injury to one of his supporters who now needs to be carried and the lack of possibility to leave him in a safe place.

4. **Conflict with his supporters** (loss or departure of one or more of them).

5. **Increase the number of obstacles** (a lot of various barriers).

6. **Increase the difficulty of obstacles** (few obstacles, however, they are almost insurmountable)

Step 6. Introduce Surprises And Unexpected Twists Into The Story

If you do this step correctly, you will not let the viewer get used to the story and let him think about anything else. When creating those surprises and twists, your objective is to make the viewer happy, surprised or scared so that you would hear things like, "Holy mackerel! Who would have thought that...," etc.

A surprise could be a revealed secret, unexpected outside assistance, meeting with a sweetheart, or betrayal of a friend at the worst possible time. It can either be pleasant or on the contrary – really aggravate the protagonist's situation.

Notes And Additional Ideas

Notes And Additional Ideas

Notes And Additional Ideas

Notes And Additional Ideas

Notes And Additional Ideas

Notes And Additional Ideas

Notes And Additional Ideas

Notes And Additional Ideas

Notes And Additional Ideas

Dear reader!

Did you receive value from STORY-FLASH WORKBOOK? Please you leave an Amazon review and share your feedback. This will help future readers choose the workbook and get benefits just like you did.

Thank you!

I wish you the best in your artistic endeavors!

May everything go your way!

Visit **Story-Flash.com** and subscribe to receive the STORY-FLASH magazine on plot development!